BLESSED

From Crazy to Cool

JASMINE LOVE

Illustration by Trevor McGary

authorHOUSE®

AuthorHouse™
1663 Liberty Drive
Bloomington, IN 47403
www.authorhouse.com
Phone: 833-262-8899

Published by AuthorHouse 10/01/2020

ISBN: 978-1-6655-0139-2 (sc)
ISBN: 978-1-6655-0258-0 (e)

Print information available on the last page.

This book is printed on acid-free paper.

Contents

Who I am, and Where I am

I am holding Isabella and smiling. I'm here to take you on a journey. A journey through body, mind, and soul. It is not a journey for the faint-hearted; It may make you turn away at times. There have been many "trials and tribulations" as is said sometimes. It is life. Life with psychic disruption AKA Mental Illness. How can I be expected to prescribe to this title of mental illness when impeccable speech is a priority?

I am now 40 years old.

Since the age of 30 I have been diagnosed with BiPolar, Schizophrenia, and Abnormal Psychosis all on separate occasions, as well as Schizotypal Personality Disorder.

My spiritual state of self-actualization was ignited in the same year as the first diagnosis.

An interesting and frightening parallel. The state of total bliss and cosmic alignment on August 8th of 2008 (8-8-8) was initiated by my yoga teacher Dharma Mittra, and the first BiPolar(Manic) Episode was in Art Basel on December 6th 0f the same year...Many of my Abnormal Psychoses and Manic Episodes were expressed during following Decembers.

There have been great inspirational states over the past 10 years; and certain deviations from normal in psychic states.

I should mention I'm a medium. I can smell people's eating habits, many times people's "essences" move through me involuntarily. It's really quite disturbing truthfully. I write from the humblest place in my heart. I don't understand all there is to know about Mental Health. My therapist at this time says that Flexibility is Mental Health. I Digg it. Flexibility is relevant to well being.

At the start of writing this body of work, I am a mother of 2 in this human dance this time around. This lifetime has had a strong EKG. So alive I am, this is a miracle.

Joy, love, and gratitude fuel me most of the time. God is within me, around me, and guides me. I am a love warrior and I practice TrueBalance Mind Body Soul Training. I practice daily meditation, exercise, journaling, sound eating, and good sleep. I also take prescription medication daily to help me ground, and to only hear and see the things that are behooving to my balance and wellbeing. Taking medication also keeps the courts and hospitals out of my life experience.

In 2016 toward my seventh month of pregnancy with my second child Isabella, I chose to get off of my medication for the pregnancy and had a Bipolar Episode, which I now call a Consciousness Crisis; I left my husband, and Aizhea (my firstborn son) was taken from me by DCF (Department of Children and Families). It was a complicated time for all of us. Aizhea was 2 years old at the time. When Isabella was born, she was taken from me at the hospital, 3 days after she was born. It was truly appalling. Admittedly I was manic, grandiose, and paranoid. I feel I handled it well considering. I looked at the psychiatrist who was present and said, "Now is when I freak out!". His face dropped with sincerity. It was an appalling moment, the kind you react to in a movie. To have lived being separated from my newborn still haunts me. I look at her sometimes and I am sad. I've learned that a good remedy for sadness is singing. My devotion to God has given me a great sounding voice. It has been said it's soothing when I speak,

Singing is courageous, just as God is courageous. I call God "The Dear One". It is a close blessed relationship I welcome with the Dear One.

Mental Health as I understand it, is the functionality of the body, the mind, the emotions, and the soul. When all operate together in a purposeful and fulfilling way, we are great. When one part deviates, we are deflated and discouraged or we are in false confidence.

I now understand that the psychic deviations with heightened spiritual states were just part of the process of my service on this planet. I am in acceptance of the process. I am blessed. The path of leadership on this rocky planet is astoundingly sacrificial. I am resolved to share my experience and teachings from and for balance. For 20 years I have been sharing the idea application called TrueBalance. It is a Yin Yang approach to humanity. Mental and Emotional Health through movement. I am blessed and privileged to share this approach with those receptive to growth, evolution, and joy into 'normalcy'. My uniqueness brings me into normalcy, as we are all unique.

Uniqueness and sameness are equally important. As I see it, they both contribute to inner and world peace. We are all patches on the same quilt of consciousness. If we all show up for our dharma (life's purpose) we can collectively play on this planet unified.

Aizhea says, "Please write my name? Will you? May you?" Now reunified, we gently engage each other into our dharma and rejoice in the progress. This is my dream for myself and the planet. Everyone at their best.

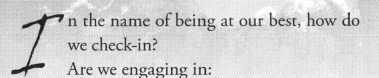

Our Best

*I*n the name of being at our best, how do we check-in?
Are we engaging in:

> Proper eating
> Proper rest
> Exercise
> Journaling
> Meditation

Daily?

In my program, we also learn to check in with the needs for:

> Focus
> Alignment

Acceptance
Peace
Vitality
Power
Flexibility
Strength
Heart Opening

We achieve these states with movement mediations.

Each area has a type of exercise that corresponds (Kickboxing, Pilates, and Yoga). These are named Zen In Ten. We administer it, in small doses to be at our best daily. Please contact me for the The Zen In Ten Collection in video format.

I am describing what works for me, and those that have trained with me. I am not pitching TrueBalance or Zen In Ten. I am sharing what has assisted me in being grateful and willing to keep growing and appreciating this life experience.

In addition to TrueBalance, I have applied and shared The Work of Byron Katie with inquiry into the mind. This is also a suggestion to loosen some beliefs that are holding us back, and discover more space in the real estate of the mind. At this point, we can choose beliefs that better resonate with are soul. And so, a mind and body challenge it is. I have realized that challenging the body and mind gives us access to our soul experience. Let us choose together these mind-body challenges deliberately, in order to then be in alignment with Grace and possibility. Drop the old story, and edit your preferences into your daily life.

I am blessed to be able to share this knowledge, these skills, and this possibility. The possibility of being empowered and in charge of our lives regardless of diagnosis or not. Between the acceptance and placebo effect of taking medication, healthy social support, and adherence to the 5 main categories previously mentioned I am ready for life.

It is possible to stay engaged with the world around us and be very high vibration. Acceptance and perseverance prevail. The application of purposeful skills is paramount and necessary for daily success. It's a daily application, just like daily medication management.

Self Awareness

The Inspiration to write this book comes from source: Within me, around me, for me, and from me. I am blessed to still be alive and generally thriving. I am an abundant flow of goodness. Everywhere I have been, I have learned and shared, I think that is what we are here to do.

Hospitalized against my will 15 times, for mental deviations of consciousness (episodes), Never hurting anyone or myself. I was fictitiously accused of doing outrageous things. I never had a knife at Aventura Hospital. I never even thought of jumping off the balcony at Grove Isle. I never threw a 60-pound object at my father. It was a pair of glasses.

Horrific! All of it. Lot's of learning. I'm on

the fast track of evolution. It's no joke. I smile to myself peacefully with the didgeridoo sound in my headphones. Peace and acceptance permeate me. I also admit that I was definitely not in an ordinary perspective when these hospitalizations occurred. I was presenting in strange ways, and my communication was limited. My behavior was also incongruent and fear based. Definitely there was also paranoia, which pushed me away from all of my loved ones. I guess I was sick, I was not in control of my attention point. It is so hard to accept that we are truly not ok. For good reason, humanity can be so lost in the understanding that those of us that have mental health issues are still of value, we don't necessarily need to be put away, shipped out, and hidden from the rest of society. In a Consciousness Crisis I am filled with many emotions simultaneously, without medication I am a mess. I offer great compassion and forgiveness to myself to let go of the past and arrive in the here and now uncluttered.

Knowing Grace

I understand now that I am a powerful, generous spirit. My presence has always been clear and inspiring. I remember all of my episodes and that is not common. My story over the past 10 years just indicates some need for support, therefore I agree with the prescribed medication. I also very much appreciate their existence, I don't prefer this awareness of the unseen. It was just part of the package of self-actualization. 52,000 psychic channels to manage, all open. I could have chosen to stay closer to my yoga teacher, there were many variables to consider at the time. So I didn't. I had to teach myself how to manage these new awarenesses. My best conclusion has been to focus on love and gratitude, and grace; rejoicing that there are medications that have been developed to yield a fulfilling exciting life. It gives me choice and control over the frequency that I vibrate at. Bye bye delusions! Hello loving integrated life! Celebrating sharing and understanding together is so nourishing.

In 2009 I didn't eat or sleep for 2 weeks. I also met the Dear One during that time.

His presence is and was so courageous. Courageously neutral and fiercely loving in the face and presence of (what humans consider) the Opponent. He blended himself lovingly with the opposing force.

It is my aim to be this essence while in this body this lifetime.

Many people with Mental Illness have strong relationships and theories about God (the Dear One). We all want to know the Dear One's presence.

God is the only true salvation. This generator of love is what makes life possible.

I am blessed to share this life with family, friends, and associations now. That is one of the indicators of true mental health. When I've been in "awareness influxes" or "episodes" my ability to communicate, relate, and trust breaks down.

When I'm taking medicine, eating properly, sleeping properly, meditating, journaling, and exercising regularly I can share life easily with others.

I feel that mental health has everything to do with being engaged at the moment. It has to do with being engaged in life. If we are fully engaged and invested in the moment, an inner joy and peace comes through. We are here now, and when we meditate we learn that our competence always shows through. Being alive, alert, and relaxed is the best way to be of service and feel good. Feeling good tells us we are on the right track.

This is not to say that we must always feel good to be healthy. It is natural to feel fatigued, sad, and irritable at times. This is all part of being human. An EKG has high parts and low parts; If it was all the same, we would be flatlined. It is in the peaks and valleys that we discover the journey. The key is to walk the middle path, not too high and not too low. TrueBalance is one way to learn how to live in balance and experience this human dance with Grace and acceptance.

We acknowledge and release stress, we receive joy, and we engage our bodies and minds in the moment. I wonder how many times I will write "I am blessed" while writing this book.

I am blessed to know and share these tools for the enlightened walk on planet Earth.

It is by sharing that I grow and receive, so I thank you for reading these words and receiving my message.

It is a great privilege to direct my own journey and lead others back to themselves.

I hold great power over my own experience and my own perspective. Through support, medicine management, and diligent healthy choices I am in the driver's seat of my experience.

When we are disengaged we feel hopeless and lost. We feel futile, ineffective, and lonely.

In today's world, there are a lot of "should's" available. There is a great lie that we "have to" do such and such and this and that. We have become slaves to our agreements and victims of circumstance. In truth, there are always choices in life.

When we are caring for ourselves properly, we can see these choices and we can have the confidence and courage to take healthy leaps. When we are leaping it gives us enthusiasm, and synchronicity lines up with us to support our gumption. It is especially important to care for ourselves properly during these times (of leaping) to remain focused, grounded, and at peace.

The Emotional Experience

*I*n order to show up moment by moment: how to show up in the world and be of true service, we must take good care of our bodies, our minds, and our souls. There are many ways and techniques for how to do this. In this book, we are contributing TrueBalance. The path of TrueBalance is broad, and it includes the tools previously mentioned.

Our emotions are an important part of navigating mental health. It's about peacefully celebrating all of the emotions that move through us throughout our lives. If we make healthy space for all of the emotions and accept them all as temporary, we can flow with life at peace. We can even accept and feel peace while noticing irritability. It will pass. All passes, all is temporary with the exception of the Ever-present Dear One.

I am blessed to share this perspective with you. In my research, I've discovered that the true definition of a psychiatrist is "a perspective doctor". He/She who studies perspective and recommends certain medicines to assist those with unique perspectives to be able to meet the world in the here and now at peace. I am grateful for all of the good and bad psychiatrists that have crossed my path.

Some diagnosed me in 30 seconds, others took the time to ask questions, and those deemed me as undiagnosable. These days I accept the support of the medicine that I take.

These temporary states of sadness and joy, etc. are like waves. They come and go. I think bipolar is an attachment to the extreme ends of the spectrum. We feel alive, enthusiastic, and confident in mania, then we feel we deserve a punishment with the following depression, and it drains our life force. That is why the regular practice of healthy behaviors strengthens us to navigate the ocean of existence as a human.

Our intensity, our primal selves need acknowledgment and healthy expression.

Therefore I recommend some boxing or martial arts for everyone who is able-bodied. Some people find a healthy alternative like chopping wood or lifting weights to make room for this part of themselves.

Either way, it is important for this part of ourselves to have space to express itself. When we don't express this part of ourselves in a healthy way, it gets expressed in impatience, irritability, and rage toward others (blaming occurs); we also direct this frustration inward blaming ourselves and getting depressed.

This part of my approach is crucial. We need space to vent in a healthy way.

Our emotions are simply indicators. Firstly, they remind us that we are human. If they are unpleasant emotions, they alert us to redirect our actions and attention. When we become keen on our indicators, we have the power to shift it. We can drink a glass of water or go for a walk if we find we are feeling emotionally out of control. Basic loving acts can shift us into grace and gratitude.

If they are pleasant emotions, this indicates to us that we are on the right path. Whatever variables are present before the good mood are variables we want to repeat. For example, if we had a good meal and went for a walk, and then we were feeling good, we would take note of what we ate and maybe keep going for walks.

I have said for decades, "The ingredients change from day to day, we must vary our remedies to be in balance".

Once again, flexibility in healthy choices is important in applying these suggestions.

As life arises, we can plan, but we are put to the test when plans change. When life's plan differs from our own we are given the opportunity to resist or adapt. When we adapt successfully we are experiencing advanced human expression.

As an example, we plan on developing our career while the children are at school, and one gets ill. We are invited and strongly urged to switch gears. We are as a woman, asked to access our nurturing and selfless action instead of progressing professionally. I breathe and realize all is well. My daughter will get better and that I have time and a willingness to write this book while she rests.

I am grateful.

How to have the Gumption to act Purposefully and Mindfully

ou feel like taking a nap. Life has been hectic and you see a pocket of time available to lay down:

1) know yourself
   and
2) know your options

1) knowing oneself-will a nap actually make me feel more rested?
   (that is the goal of a healthy nap)
2) knowing your options
   a) stretching

b) moving a meaningful project along
c) eating or drinking something energizing

This way we access how to procceed from a place of choice.

Small steps lead to great victories. Remember, you and I have chosen this journey, and we continue to show up voluntarily as examples for those around us. Don't co-sign mediocrity for yourself. Take small steps to stay honest, open-minded, and willing in your journey. Willing to be in and be the progress on Planet Earth.

Taking good care of yourself and your affairs frees up space for inspired thoughts, which can lead to progressive action.

This is all then service. We are built for service. We serve in many different ways. We can serve our country. We can serve humanity. We can serve the Dear One. In service, we are to our families. In service, we are to the Beloved (Dear One) in everyone.

Being the example of His Qualities Includes Equanimity, Tranquility, Mercy, Patience, Grace, Mirth, Focus, Stern, Clarity, Sincerity, Humility, Humor, Joy, and Vigor.

It is a passionate, loving, peaceful expression, that is the goal. If we choose this path the rewards are huge: Fulfillment, Purpose, Joy for the sake of it, and gratitude, not to mention a deeper peace.

Self Realization

We embark on a journey into ourselves. Our actualized selves.

It's a privilege to share this journey with you. It is my aim to share insights and inspiration with others that dance and/or fight with mental illness. It is my aim to redirect our language and align us with true mental health.

Each person is an individual. Therefore, each individual's most important variable is that they remain engaged with their own programming. Complete programming consists of Body, Mind, and Soul. All three areas are relevant and equally important.

How will you take good care of yourself today?

How will we rise to the occasion of life?

What steps need we take to stay willing and excited about life?

There are daily tasks that are more joyfully experienced when we have meditated and exercised that day. Transitioning with skill, grace, and certainty that all is well from task to task. Fluidity is a component of the previously mentioned flexibility.

The intention of generosity and expanded gratitude building between us is crucial.

Now knowing how and when to connect with each other impeccably and with grace, gentleness, and understanding.

I am blessed to share my process with you.

I can feel a great deal of the ethereal. Due to a strong bond with The Dear One for a long time. I hold a deep intention to be in the solution, to be in love, to be in grace, ease, wholeness, and wellness. To show up as my best in every possible way while I'm here.

Mental Illness has been a gift. It has "strongly urged" me to pay closer attention to what I am experiencing more than most. It has led me deep into the steps, tasks, and healthy, smart choices that keep me engaged with the world.

The ethereal and the terrestrial are of equal importance as a human.

Breath and body in unison are of priority.

We must have both to be who we came to be while reading these words. That one shining you.

I love the movie I have lived. Should I be graced with long life, the future is filled with beauty, joy, and rejoicing. I am blessed and determined.

I can only get better at life. Through applied knowledge, technique implementation, and shared experience.

Grateful for the willingness to share. Being at True Peace is somewhat unfamiliar. It is reprogramming and adjustment to freedom. Knowing all is well and trusting in the stillness. The depth of True Peace is in Trust. Trust in our own capacity, and trust in the process.

When we share from true peace, there is no adding or taking away, there is simply shared consciousness.

True Peace is completeness in itself. From wholeness, we are majestic mountains with thriving bio-systems all within. We are whole and sustainable, emotionally sober, and content. From contentment, we can serve. When we are at peace we can collaborate joyfully. Making space for others' contributions with openness and receptivity to the unified expression.

Agendas are no longer relevant. The expression in itself is enough. Fulfillment occurs in giving and receiving, in sharing our knowledge, enthusiasm, and support.

Interpersonal relations are paramount for mental health. We experience interconnected acknowledgment, relating, humor, and encouragement in healthy relations. This in itself can heal us from the stigma of mental illness residue that we have experienced while being sick.

Engagement with life's tasks, as well as engagement with people around us is relevant.

Sensual and sexual health is also relevant.

Meditation, exercise, and prayer assist with these areas. Engagement mentally and physically is more accessible after we have meditated and exercised. We are in our "yes" zone. "Yes" to the moment, yes to life. Life occurs at this moment. "Yes" to the possibility of progress embodied. When we are in our own "yes" zone, the action is possible. When action is possible, depression is less prevalent.

Some would argue that this "yes" zone is a

manic state. I think the attachment to the highs in life is more of an accurate description of mania. Mania lacks access to the middle line. The "yes" zone is a deliberate choice of consciousness and right action.

The breath is also a way to move our experience.

To be present to the possibility and space within the moment, we breathe and align our joints.

This is why we train and practice daily. So that these skills develop naturally through training and practice effect.

We accustom our system to breathe fully and fluidly, and our joints align, more effectively and effortlessly when we exercise regularly.

The Mind is then freed up to respond to and with the moment effectively (with encouragement and love).

Gratitude is then accessible and shared. When we are in gratitude, we are in our wisdom. We can appreciate all that unfolds within us, around us, for us, and from us as part of the process of learning and living.

Prayer allows us to accept this unfolding with courage and peace. Being at peace gives us space to live freely in the moment. Peace is not perfection, it allows us acceptance with the highs and lows. We are grounded and certain of the temporary nature of life experience. Therefore, we allow the unfolding to occur with grace and resolve. Certainty in our capacity is made accessible by meditating daily. Once we have meditated we are in contact with the Dear One within and around us, and the day unfolds with greater ease and grace.

We are constantly healing and learning. It is wonderful. We are in the learning of how to serve as humans, and to be love to one another and ourselves.

Freedom facilitates love. When we are free, our attention can be directed to loving, serving, and sharing.

Gratitude, prayer, and exercise facilitate willingness

By the Grace of God, I write these words and surrender to the Grace in all of us. Humor and connection are ours to share.

Grateful for the communication with myself enough to have insight and share my truth.

My truth involves love, courage, and grace. With the raw willingness to show up, I show up again and again.

Wisdom exudes through me to know how to show up in the world. My aim is to be present and share a secure, sound, and inspiring experience. True Freedom is in congruence with the breath. Freedom is grounded in truth moment by moment. Grace is in every breath.

Navigating Relationships

*E*ven when we are uncomfortable, even when we are sick, Grace is with us. We can gently bring our attention point to Grace in the moment, to encouragement, love, and gratitude. Humility and confidence yield meaningful relationships. Meaningful relationships keep us integrated and directed.

If someone is agreeable with us, we feel accepted, which is wonderful.

Conversely, if someone is disagreeable with us, we deepen our resolve toward our position, our truth. Our inner radar is sometimes spunky; someone says, "You can't do that!" and the inner radar says, "Wanna bet?" We tame the spunk into a constructive resolution to know and follow through with our truth, our mission. We accept suggestions from ourselves and gracefully from others. We receive and adapt along the journey.

The biggest obstacle we face is ourselves. We have been rejected by ourselves and others time and time again. We push away our uniqueness and try to understand the ways of the world.

From one enlightened being to another, we know that all is well always here and now.

Every circumstance has a solution, one moment at a time.

Peaceful Acceptance

*A*cceptance is a major variable to consider and explore when mental health is relevant. Self-acceptance and acceptance of others are allowed in good mental health. We know our strengths and the places that challenge us. Through acceptance, we can see more clearly the nature of the obstacle and administer a solution with more clarity.

Self-management (with collaboration) is the invitation. Bring it, and take good care of yourself. Break it down to a moment by moment.

Acceptance is also a vital aspect of true mental health. Knowing when to ask for support, and have acceptance is a game-changer. When we let go and become humble, we have greater confidence and ease communicating authentically and effectively. We are heard and our needs can be better met. Grace is with us.

Presentation and Dignity

*A*nother aspect of great relevance to this subject is caring for our appearance. It is an act of love to present ourselves deliberately in the world. We are respecting ourselves enough to put time and energy into our presentation

When we present ourselves with dignity, the world treats us as such. We also can feel more confident, when we have put ourselves together deliberately. We move with more certainty in this way. Moving with certainty affirms our wellness to ourselves and others. Therefore, strengthening our relationships. When we have stronger relationships, we have greater support. With ample support, we have access to love, acceptance, and opportunity. When these variables are in place, we are engaged with life. By being engaged, mental health is with us. We feel effective, relevant, and peacefully joyful. What a delight!

We've gone through what we've gone through to be better where we are.

The past is a gift, the present is a miracle, and the future is awesome! Life is full of surprises, be present as the miracle to embrace them with grace and peace.

Know your priorities and live for them. Show up with these priorities leading your journey. Tons of willingness, creativity, connectedness, and fulfillment is on the other side. You deserve, you are grace, you are a miracle. Be the miracle and have the courage to do what it takes to feel long term goodness. Be someone you want to wake up and go to bed with.

Through my separation from my husband, I "dated myself" on several occasions. Courting myself and loving myself along the way. Some nights I would place the full-length mirror facing me in bed, just to tell myself "good morning, I love you!" It was precious.

Be Yourself

How to be ourselves and be in the world as it is:

Rejoice in the little successes

"Put down the bat, and give yourself a pat"

Move your body and breathe deliberately

Know when to engage, and when to let go.

Learn to relax effectively.

Remember "The past is a gift, the present is a miracle, and the future is AWE-SOME"

Be in the awe-some-ness.

Be in nature daily.

Pay attention

Look for ways to be of service.

Count your blessings.

Express Gratitude Overtly-use your words to create an expansion of gratitude.

These pointers are crucial for being willing and healthy: We accept life as it unfolds. In Grace, we are able to contribute meaningfully and effectively: We live out what is important to us.

How do we know when to rest and let go, and when to take action?

Own your body as a home for the soul.

Ask for guidance and let in supportive, encouraging relations.

Note suggestions and then hold priorities up in your consciousness to then execute your next move.

Work collaboratively with others to let the momentum continue without your direct involvement.

Delegate and appreciate

Check-in on the purpose of your choices-what are the intentions behind your choices-before you elect a given behavior...pause and align: your purpose, intention, and priorities.

Nature is gentle and full of Grace, and so we are invited to be gentle as well.

Gentle Mentally, Physically, and Emotionally. We are invited to be swift and graceful in our existence. We devote ourselves to our highest good by remaining clear on what's important to us and then showing up for it. We are encouraged to gently redirect our attention point to that which we'd like to see more of. Just as we would with a young child. If peace and ease are priorities, watch a television show about nature or listen to relaxing music instead of watching something dramatic and/or chaotic. Choose behaviors that align with what's important to you.

My Personal Unfolding

Let's get a bit more personal:
I'm a very open-minded and open-hearted woman.

At the time of initially writing this book, it seemed I was going to divorce my husband. It is now 2 years later and we are very much unified as a couple and a family. From that time until now there has been immense growth and enjoyment together. What I brought my attention to in that difficult period was accepting myself as is; emotional and physical development in my partner (at the time I did not imagine that my husband would end up being that man) At the time of first handwriting this book, I gratefully released the relationship knowing deeply that through the pleasant and the unpleasant, the relationship had been of service to me in a myriad of ways.

My children are very important to me. I am in ongoing awe of the miracles that they are. They are both magnificent.

The three of us carry the last name, Love. We all love it. My children honor and value love and everything that comes with it. Including my husband, he has his birth given last name. Together we are the LOVE squad.

My firstborn child named Robert Aizhea Love, goes by Aizhea Love (this is a play on words sounding out, "I is LOVE"! Love is gentle, love IS patient. Love is caring, Love is expansion, Love is Renewing. LOVE is a Possibility.

My second child named Isabella Marie Love goes by Bella Love. When we say, Isabella Love, we are also saying, "It's a Bella". Beauty is present to bring about inspiration. Beauty could even be celebrating God's proven magnificence. It encourages us to keep going. To put a skip in our step. In life, we have a choice on our attention point. Knowing that I am here to be of service reminds me to keep it simple.

One moment at a time, I engage in the experience.

I was loving, honoring, and respecting myself when I was considering a divorce. I nourished and cherished myself, as I would my own children. I am and was present for friends with a thirst to know love and the Dear One. A thirst for meaning and wholeness. My generation (baby boomer's kids) has a lot of reprogramming to harness. Our children are here to teach us and remind us of what's important. Service, balance, and gratitude are core values at the root of those that are awake and that chose well being and grace in this life.

As we learn, we get strong through peace and capacity.

I practice my attention point with the statement, "In the silence is the voice of my soul".

We can rest in the quiet warmth of the Dear One that permeates it all. We then know all is well.

Once we feel all is well we have the accessibility to respond gracefully with strength, patience, peace, and humor.

It adds more depth, texture, and poetry to my story, the trials, and tribulations that I have risen above. One of which was an "almost" divorce in 2017, for which I felt and transcended great emotional pain. At the time, I was able to see that Trevor was a man I had been wholeheartedly devoted to. I am constantly looking for meaning, purpose, and service, and my perspective yields a magical life, and ordinary life of joy, love, and possibility. Abundant surprises are constantly popping up.

Adversity is not new to me. I have been Baker Acted over 15 times. I can feel the wave of reactive emotions just as I bring my attention to this topic. So I will be brief and concise. A Baker Act is when someone chooses to have you detained in the hospital for 72 hours and observed psychiatrically under the assumption that you are a danger to yourself or others.

My chest hurts as I write this portion. I am resolved to make a positive impact in the world. My resolve is to manifest through my children, my now solid marriage with Trevor, and a diverse career. Patience in Namaste is what I practiced then in 2017, and now in 2020 I continue to walk at the Pace of Grace. With Receptivity and Love, I proceed to connect with Possibilty and Understanding.

Let's come clean!

As of 2017, I had not been financially successful

in my career. I guess I had been blocked, Too Proud I guess. Maybe even unapproachable. I am shifting my awareness into possibility consistently, as well as generosity. Generosity with myself and others. Present to serve.

Humbled, diligent, and honest I proceed with playfulness on this treacherous planet. Discerning one moment at a time what to expound upon. My heart feels better. I am released into the unknown of transformation.

I am blessed in new and exciting ways. Diligent and enthusiastic I apply my knowledge daily.

Daily is the key.

Daily, moment by moment, assessing how to serve in love.

How to be in love with life: choose goodness on every level.

Let go of judgment and criticism. Release yourself into the moment.

When a wave of heavy feelings are moving through, pause, and asses this:

Focus on what you CAN do right now:

Make a list and refer to it continuously throughout the day and always.

Express yourself creatively:

       sing
       dance
       move
       write

converse
Give.

Remember your infinite true nature, accept the rest as temporary. Breath. Let Go Now

Be honest with yourself and others.

Be Gentle.

Rock it.

I am grateful to be of service in sharing my truth.

Let's say "Yes" to life together. Accept the Challenges as Opportunities and move along. We remain willing and keen on the next right step. Becoming worthy and collaborating with others on this experience called "life". When we are suffering, remembering it is temporary we have the capacity to ask for and receive help and support. We also have the capacity to be of service when we acknowledge and accept our own suffering as temporary.

Another way to stay engaged is to ask ourselves the question, "How would the Dear One respond?"

"I am Love" is a great affirmation for wholeness and fulfillment.

Remembering what is important to me carries

and encourages me through any new trials and tribulations with patience and connectivity. It makes space for enthusiasm and excitement about the future.

Courage is called upon to see, acknowledge, and express painful emotions. We can then find constructive ways to experience life. Pray for gentleness, and deliberately execute action lovingly and peacefully.

Faith is called on to carry us through.

The Evolution of the Language Associated with Mental Illness

*H*ow to rename our "conditions"?

There is a thirst I have for renaming the diagnoses in clinical psychology. I feel acceptance and encouragement need to be at the root of these categories.

The stigmas and vibrations of the current names of the Disorders in Mental Health are destructive and paralyzing. They are fear and panic based. They also contribute to the denial of the patient when attempting to accept their particular issue.

Let's move from acceptance and love of our

uniqueness instead. Celebrating and calibrating true threats to our safety as humanity.

I meditated deeply and walked extensively during my episodes. I did not feel safe, secure, or loved. I felt alone.

I was being shown ethereal aspects that don't make sense. I am still applying forgiveness for these deviations from sanity and psychotic breaks. I understand now that my loved ones didn't understand, and neither did I. We didn't understand what was happening. I now understand that my soul is ambitious and that my spirit signed up to clear all of that ethereal garbage that I came in contact with.

What would we rename the term, "Psychotic"??? It is defined as seeing or hearing things that others cannot verify. Vibrationally the term psychotic is just freaky. Let's try the term "dIstracted sight or sound" or DSS. When someone is experiencing Psychosis or DSS they are not focused, and they are difficult to connect with.

While my soul knows that there is nothing to gain or lose in this journey, that the whole is already complete, my human self is reminded to release the need to compare myself with others.

With Insight, I realize my "work" has been

more prominent in the unseen. Being Jasmine Love means the verifiable external gain is irrelevant. The quality of my experience is relevant. How I feel and others feel around me is what is relevant.

For someone previously diagnosed as BiPolar, Schitzophrenic, Abnormal Psychosis, I sure had a warm and fulfilling Superbowl party in 2017 when I began writing this book. I now have a rich life, filled with many loving relationships. This includes my nuclear family, spouse, and children.

Life is Good. The future is full of delightful surprises, thanks to my willingness and the Grace of the Dear One. Love works.

Choice

To be confident, calm, and accepting is a choice. I am blessed to live a free life with fulfillment available constantly. My tools absolutely work. I trust myself and I am free.

My work is necessary and enriching for all involved. I am blessed and grateful for the capacity and access to the greatness that lives and breaths me.

This life is full of inspiration and possibility. I am a divine conduit and an example of this magnificence.

I receive with grace, poise, and worthiness. When I receive everybody wins. I am disciplined and playful with everything that is shared with me. I am a blessing. I contribute meaningfully, I am fierce, precise, and certain of my positive contribution today. Engaged and in love, Gratitude fills and expands with me.

Remember that vigor. It is a certain quality of God and nature.

Go get it, be it, feel it.

Suit up and deliver with effortless ease and capacity. Keep breathing and flowing. There is so much to share.

Be willing. Step into your truth, breath by breath. Smile from your soul and move.

Move into the greatness of this experience. Receive, and give it.

Remember that service looks and feels different daily and individually.

Being receptive to Grace means slowing down and rejoicing in the little things with bliss and appreciation.

Once our exercise and meditation are completed and accomplished, we can access this peaceful bliss in life's little treasures.

Our mechanism is then vibrating in a place of ease and willingness to once again engage in life and deliver.

Notice the power of choice. Engage in behavior that behooves you and your purpose.

Choose life. Choose to live and embrace the journey of creation.

Be wild within the boundaries of tame, and express your pure, infinite self. Let your joy permeate your body, and say "yes" to creation. Smile quietly and loudly and always peacefully. Know you were created to contribute constructively. Practice compassion with the parts of you that don't believe this, and nurture those parts into a willingness to see and be grounded in truth. You are loved. The universe is constantly affirming it for you. Pause long enough to receive the love that is you, and receive the richness of the everlasting present. Remember you are a miracle just as you are. Celebrate this fact in your own unique way. Smile and rejoice in trust. Trust that all is well in that breath. The infinite lives there, in the breath.

Remember that feedback from others, whether favorable or not is a reflection of their own experience. Understanding through effective expression and communication is available when we are allowing our true selves to show up. Our true selves are available in the breath. Joy is a river that can be cultivated through good self-care.

Even if we are having discouraging emotions, we can rejoice to know they are temporary, and that all emotions contribute to creation.

When we choose evolution and personal development our emotional expression shifts from a "heavy metal band" to a "symphony". We are able to identify skillfully with the breath instead of the emotions. We breathe in grace and give permission for the emotions to move through. Our mind is the conductor. Directing attention and identification with the breath.

Perform the next right task in grace. Make space for grace to show up in your relations, your tasks, and all of life's moments. For grace is everpresent. As humans we have free will; we can either receive in union with ease and knowing, or we can separate and doubt. To know in grace is heaven. We are all here to remind each other of how safe we really are; And that all is well. Embodied grace. That's it. Meditation and exercise yields this state.

The Magic of Meditation and Exercise

 *J*oy is our natural state. The main blocks for joy are misunderstanding and resentment. Sometimes it is required to choose resentment or gratitude. Gratitude is a grace vibration. We misunderstand ourselves, our needs, our purpose, even our contribution. We misunderstand each other and the world around us.

When we are in Joy, all is right with the world. To access our joy we must have discipline. The discipline to take good care of ourselves, our homes, our cars, our businesses, our earth, and each other. How do we take care of ourselves?

By exercising, resting, eating-, meditating,

and journaling. Journaling grounds us and gives us an outlet to express and understand ourselves.

In order to understand each other, communication must be gentle, compassionate, and courageous. We must learn to listen effectively to each other. We must breathe deeply and seek to hear and understand without judgment or competition. Relating with one another gently and soulfully. Wholeheartedly reciprocating vulnerability and grace. When accessing joy through good self-care, we are in our power, and therefore, communication enhances our connection. Our power is not depleted by the other party because our natural state of wellbeing is strong. Solutions and Insights are available due to our meditation state, and contentment is ours.

When communicating, chose to be in your breath and listen. Be alert to clues to understand each other. Look for similarities in each other. Look for opportunities to confirm understanding. Take responsibility for your part in the topic being discussed, and proceed to make space for grace. Be willing to learn about yourself and others. Be receptive to progress and transformation. In grace, there is space for understanding. When we understand, we heal. When we heal, we are in infinite possibility. Within that possibility lies insight. With insight, there is creativity, love, acceptance, and connection. There are humor and playfulness as well.

All is well, and life is a celebration, learning, and becoming.

Acceptance, peace, and enthusiasm are real, accessible, and available.

Embrace yourself fully and experience grace. Unconditional access to Love.

By way of the breath, we steady the mind on the gift of now.

Sometimes life can feel overwhelming. In those times, self-care is paramount. It is crucial to let ourselves be supported, and bring ourselves back to ease.

Love is such a gentle presence. Let's release the labels and receive the reality that all is well. Let's implement language impeccably. Let's also identify any victim or lack based thoughts and smile. Administer your attention point to compassion and identify with the breath. Know that your soul, what makes us who we are, is infused into the breath. Focus on three breaths. I am love, I release all else.

The Surrender: Letting Go

Specifically control, shame, guilt, and self-victimization. All of these are illusions of the mind. Once "shoulding" is released, we elect empowered and grateful behavior. We promote creation moving through us. Once the vessel of the mind, body and soul is unburdened by the agendas of others and even our own egos, we have true freedom. Freedom to savor each moment and receive the everlasting love of the universe.

The lessons and opportunities for growth will continue.

If we meet the moment with love we are consistently nourished. Blessed to be alive we proceed in peace and go about being our true selves.

Relaxed, present, and amazed by life's infinite gifts.

In peaceful enthusiasm, we are participating in a steady stream of goodness.

I should update you! (reader)

I have now reconciled with my husband, thanks to the power of love, diligence, and healing.

(When handwriting these words) it was June 3rd, 2018, and we reconciled as of March 5, 2018.

Yesterday we celebrated our 5 year wedding anniversary. We chose to mutually participate in weekly 30-minute healings together and hold a financial meeting for 30 minutes after our healing time. So far, so magnificent!

Very grateful! Peacefully receiving constantly.

The challenges are not here to offend us, they arrive or emerge when we're ready to learn and meet them with love.

Acknowledging that happiness is a choice, is a game-changer.

Giving ourselves permission to smile on the inside during challenges defines our character.

Instead of getting bitter, we choose to be

better. Better examples of grace manifest. Be blessed continually.

Meet the moment with courage and be ok with it.

Printed in the United States
By Bookmasters